Confidence Building for Kids: A Guide to Building Confidence and Self-Esteem of shy children

Introduction

Shyness is a common trait among children, and it can be a significant obstacle to their social and emotional development. Shy children often struggle to make friends, participate in group activities, and express themselves. They may feel anxious or insecure in social situations, which can lead to low self-esteem and a lack of confidence.

As a parent or caregiver, it can be challenging to know how to help a shy child overcome these obstacles and build confidence. However, with patience, understanding, and the right strategies, it is possible to help shy children feel more comfortable and confident in social situations.

This book is designed to provide practical advice and strategies for parents and caregivers to help their shy children build confidence and overcome their shyness. By following the guidance in this book, parents and caregivers can help their children develop the social and emotional skills they need to succeed in life.

Encourage participation in activities: One of the most effective ways to help shy children build confidence is to encourage their participation in activities. Whether it's sports, music, drama, or other group activities, participation in structured activities can help children develop social skills, build self-confidence, and learn to work with others.

When encouraging participation in activities, it is important to choose activities that your child is interested in and feels comfortable with. It's also important to encourage your child to try new things and take risks, but to do so in a safe and supportive environment. By helping your child find the right activities and providing positive reinforcement, you can help them build their confidence and develop a sense of accomplishment.

Provide opportunities for socialization: Another important strategy for helping shy children build confidence is to provide opportunities for socialization. This can include playdates, group outings, and other social events where your child can interact with other children and adults.

When providing opportunities for socialization, it is important to choose events and activities that your child will enjoy and feel comfortable with. It's also important to provide support and guidance to help your child navigate social situations and develop social skills. By providing regular opportunities for socialization, you can help your child build their confidence and develop positive relationships with others.

Model confident behavior: Children often learn by example, and one of the most effective ways to help shy children build confidence is to model confident behavior yourself. This means being assertive, confident, and positive in your interactions with your child and others.

When modeling confident behavior, it is important to be aware of your own attitudes and behaviors. For example, if you are anxious or insecure in social situations, your child may pick up on these cues and become more anxious themselves. By modeling confident behavior, you can help your child develop a positive self-image and feel more comfortable in social situations.

Praise effort, not just achievement: Another important strategy for helping shy children build confidence is to praise effort, not just achievement. This means recognizing your child's efforts and progress, rather than just focusing on their accomplishments.

When praising effort, it is important to be specific and sincere in your praise. For example, instead of saying "good job," you might say "I'm proud of you for working so hard on that project." By praising effort, you can help your child develop a sense of self-worth and accomplishment, regardless of the outcome.

Teach problem-solving skills: Problem-solving skills are essential for building confidence and resilience in children. By teaching your child problem-solving skills, you can help them develop the ability to handle difficult situations and overcome obstacles.

When teaching problem-solving skills, it is important to encourage your child to think creatively and consider different solutions to problems. It's also important to provide guidance and support as your child learns these skills.

Focus on strengths: Another important strategy for helping shy children build confidence is to focus on their strengths. Every child has unique talents and abilities, and by focusing on these strengths, you can help your child develop a sense of self-worth and accomplishment.

When focusing on strengths, it is important to be specific and sincere in your praise. For example, if your child is good at art, you might say "I love the way you used color in your painting. You have a real talent for art." By focusing on strengths, you can help your child develop a positive self-image and feel more confident in their abilities.

Practice positive self-talk: Positive self-talk is a powerful tool for building confidence and self-esteem in children. By encouraging your child to use positive self-talk, you can help them develop a more positive self-image and feel more confident in their abilities.

When practicing positive self-talk, it is important to encourage your child to focus on their strengths and accomplishments, rather than their weaknesses and mistakes. You might also encourage your child to use positive affirmations, such as "I am capable," "I am strong," or "I can do this." By practicing positive self-talk, you can help your child develop a more positive mindset and feel more confident in their abilities.

Set achievable goals: Setting achievable goals is an important strategy for helping shy children build confidence. By setting goals that are challenging but achievable, you can help your child develop a sense of accomplishment and build their self-esteem.

When setting goals, it is important to involve your child in the process and make sure the goals are realistic and attainable. You might also break larger goals into smaller, more manageable steps, so your child can feel a sense of progress and accomplishment along the way. By setting achievable goals, you can help your child develop a sense of control and confidence in their ability to succeed.

Celebrate successes: Celebrating successes is an important part of building confidence in children. By acknowledging and celebrating your child's accomplishments, you can help them develop a sense of pride and confidence in their abilities.

When celebrating successes, it is important to be specific and sincere in your praise. You might also consider small rewards or incentives to reinforce positive behaviors and accomplishments. By celebrating successes, you can help your child develop a positive self-image and feel more confident in their abilities.

Create a safe and supportive environment: Creating a safe and supportive environment is essential for building confidence in children. By providing a nurturing and supportive environment, you can help your child feel safe and secure, and build their self-esteem.

When creating a safe and supportive environment, it is important to provide positive reinforcement, emotional support, and a sense of consistency and structure. You might also encourage your child to express their feelings and thoughts, and provide guidance and support as needed.

By creating a safe and supportive environment, you can help your child develop a sense of security and confidence in themselves and their abilities.

Avoid labeling your child as "shy": Labeling your child as "shy" can be counterproductive and can reinforce negative self-perceptions. Instead of labeling your child as "shy," focus on their strengths and positive qualities, and provide guidance and support as needed. By avoiding labels and focusing on positive traits, you can help your child develop a more positive self-image and feel more confident in themselves.

Offer encouragement and support: Encouragement and support are essential for building confidence in children. By providing positive reinforcement, emotional support, and a sense of guidance, you can help your child feel more confident and secure.

When offering encouragement and support, it is important to be specific and sincere in your praise, and to provide guidance and support as needed. You might also encourage your child to express their feelings and thoughts, and provide a safe and supportive environment

Teach assertiveness skills: Teaching assertiveness skills is an important strategy for helping shy children build confidence. By teaching your child to assert itself in a respectful and confident way, you can help them develop a sense of control and confidence in their ability to communicate their needs and feelings.

When teaching assertiveness skills, it is important to model assertive behavior, and provide guidance and support as needed. You might also encourage your child to practice assertiveness in safe and supportive environments, such as with close friends or family members.

By teaching assertiveness skills, you can help your child develop a sense of empowerment and confidence in their ability to communicate effectively.

Encourage risk-taking in safe environments: Encouraging risk-taking in safe environments is an important strategy for helping shy children build confidence. By encouraging your child to take risks and try new things in a safe and supportive environment, you can help them develop a sense of adventure and confidence in their abilities.

When encouraging risk-taking, it is important to provide guidance and support, and to create a safe and supportive environment where your child feels comfortable taking risks. You might also encourage your child to practice taking risks in small steps, and to celebrate their successes along the way.

By encouraging risk-taking in safe environments, you can help your child develop a sense of courage and confidence in their ability to overcome challenges.

Help your child manage anxiety: Managing anxiety is an important part of building confidence in shy children. By teaching your child coping skills and strategies for managing anxiety, you can help them feel more in control and confident in challenging situations.

When helping your child manage anxiety, it is important to provide guidance and support, and to model healthy coping strategies. You might also encourage your child to practice relaxation techniques, such as deep breathing or visualization, and to seek professional help if needed.

By helping your child manage anxiety, you can help them feel more confident and secure in themselves and their abilities.

Encourage self-expression through art or writing: Encouraging self-expression through art or writing is an important strategy for helping shy children build confidence. By providing opportunities for your child to express themselves creatively, you can help them develop a sense of self-awareness and confidence in their own unique perspectives and talents.

When encouraging self-expression, it is important to provide a safe and supportive environment, and to praise your child's efforts and creativity. You might also encourage your child to share their creations with others, or to participate in creative activities with peers.

By encouraging self-expression through art or writing, you can help your child develop a sense of self-worth and confidence in their own unique talents and perspectives.

Celebrate diversity and differences: Celebrating diversity and differences is an important strategy for helping shy children build confidence. By embracing and celebrating differences in others, you can help your child develop a sense of acceptance and tolerance, and build their self-esteem.

When celebrating diversity and differences, it is important to model inclusive and respectful behavior, and to provide opportunities for your child to learn about and appreciate different cultures, beliefs, and perspectives.

You might also encourage your child to participate in activities or events that celebrate diversity, such as cultural festivals or community service projects. By celebrating diversity and differences, you can help your child develop a sense of empathy and confidence in their ability to connect with others.

Avoid comparing your child to others: Comparing your child to others can be damaging to their self-esteem and confidence. Instead of comparing your child to others, focus on their unique strengths and qualities, and provide guidance and support as needed.

By avoiding comparisons and focusing on positive qualities, you can help your child develop a positive self-image and feel more confident in their abilities.

Foster a sense of independence: Fostering a sense of independence is an important strategy for helping shy children build confidence. By encouraging your child to take on age-appropriate responsibilities and make decisions on their own, you can help them develop a sense of autonomy and confidence in their ability to handle challenges.

When fostering independence, it is important to provide guidance and support, and to encourage your child to take on new responsibilities gradually. You might also praise your child for their efforts and accomplishments, and provide opportunities for them to learn new skills and take on new challenges.

By fostering a sense of independence, you can help your child develop a sense of confidence and self-reliance.

Seek professional help if needed: If your child is struggling with severe shyness or social anxiety, it may be helpful to seek professional help. A mental health professional can provide guidance and support, and help your child develop coping strategies for managing their anxiety and building confidence.

When seeking professional help, it is important to choose a qualified and experienced provider, and to work collaboratively with them to develop a treatment plan that meets your child's individual needs. You might also consider involving other family members or caregivers in the treatment process, to provide additional support and encouragement for your child.

Building confidence in shy children is a process that requires patience, guidance, and support. By providing opportunities for socialization, modeling confident behavior, and teaching coping strategies for managing anxiety, you can help your child develop a sense of control and confidence in their ability to navigate social situations.

Additionally, by focusing on their strengths, celebrating their successes, and avoiding comparisons to others, you can help your child develop a positive self-image and a sense of self-worth.

Ultimately, building confidence in shy children requires a commitment to creating a safe and supportive environment where they can feel comfortable taking risks, expressing themselves, and learning new skills.

With patience, guidance, and support, you can help your child develop the confidence and self-esteem they need to thrive socially and emotionally.

Encourage Participation in activities

Encouraging children to participate in activities can be a great way to boost their confidence and help them overcome shyness. Participating in activities can help children develop new skills, meet new people, and gain a sense of accomplishment.

Here are some ways to encourage participation in activities:

Start with their interests: Start by asking your child what activities they are interested in. This could be anything from sports to music to art. By starting with their interests, you are more likely to engage their enthusiasm and help them develop a sense of passion for the activity.

Find local programs: Once you know what your child is interested in, research local programs or clubs that offer those activities. For example, if your child is interested in soccer, look for local youth soccer leagues or camps.

Offer support: Encourage your child to participate in the activity and offer support along the way. This could include attending games or performances, helping them practice at home, or simply being a cheerleader for their efforts. Set achievable goals: Help your child set achievable goals related to the activity. For example, if they are learning to play the guitar, their goal could be to learn a new song each week. Achieving these goals can help build confidence and a sense of accomplishment.

Celebrate successes: Celebrate your child's successes related to the activity. This could be anything from scoring a goal to mastering a new chord on the guitar. Celebrating these successes can help your child feel proud of their accomplishments and motivated to continue.

Avoid pressure: While it's important to encourage participation in activities, it's also important to avoid putting too much pressure on your child. Avoid pushing them to be the best or comparing them to others. Instead, focus on the enjoyment of the activity and the growth that comes with practice and effort.

Make it fun: Finally, make sure the activity is fun for your child. While there may be moments of frustration or challenge, overall the activity should be enjoyable and engaging. This will help your child develop a love for the activity and a sense of confidence in their abilities.

Encouraging participation in activities can be a great way to help children gain confidence and overcome shyness.

By starting with their interests, finding local programs, offering support, setting achievable goals, celebrating successes, avoiding pressure, and making it fun, you can help your child develop a love for the activity and a sense of accomplishment.

Provide opportunities for socialization

Providing opportunities for socialization is important for children to develop social skills, build relationships, and overcome shyness. Socialization opportunities can include everything from playdates to extracurricular activities to family outings.

Here are some ways to provide opportunities for socialization:

Start with playdates: Arrange playdates with other children who your child may not have met before. This can help your child develop social skills in a safe and familiar environment. Join a club or team: Encourage your child to join a club or team that aligns with their interests. This can help them meet new people and develop a sense of community.

Attend community events: Attend community events such as festivals or fairs. This can help your child meet new people and experience new things.

Volunteer: Volunteer with your child for a local charity or organization. This can help them develop a sense of empathy and compassion, while also meeting new people.

Plan family outings: Plan outings as a family to places such as museums, parks, or amusement parks. This can help your child develop a sense of adventure and curiosity, while also spending time with family members.

Provide opportunities for free play: Provide opportunities for your child to engage in free play with other children. This can help them develop social skills and learn how to navigate social situations on their own.

When providing opportunities for socialization, it's important to keep in mind your child's individual needs and interests. Not all children are comfortable in large groups or may prefer one-on-one interactions. It's important to respect your child's preferences and provide socialization opportunities that align with their needs.

In addition, it's important to model positive social behavior for your child. This can include being friendly to others, engaging in conversation, and showing empathy and kindness. By modeling positive social behavior, you can help your child develop social skills and build positive relationships with others.

Providing opportunities for socialization can help children develop social skills, build relationships, and overcome shyness. By starting with playdates, joining clubs or teams, attending community events, volunteering, planning family outings, encouraging participation in group activities, and providing opportunities for free play, you can help your child develop social skills and confidence.

Model Confident Behavior

Modeling confident behavior is one of the most effective ways parents can help their children overcome shyness and develop confidence. Children look to their parents for guidance and support, and by modeling confident behavior, parents can help their children develop a positive self-image and a sense of self-assurance.

Here are some ways to model confident behavior:

Be positive: One of the most important things parents can do is to be positive in their interactions with their children. This means avoiding negative comments or criticisms and instead focusing on positive feedback and encouragement.

Practice assertiveness: Modeling assertive behavior can help children learn to express themselves and their needs in a confident way. This means speaking up for oneself and setting boundaries in a clear and respectful way.

Take care of yourself: Taking care of oneself is an important part of modeling confidence. This means practicing self-care, such as exercise, healthy eating, and adequate rest. It also means prioritizing one's own needs and making time for activities that bring joy and fulfillment.

Embrace challenges: Modeling a willingness to take on challenges can help children learn to embrace new experiences and overcome their fears. This means trying new things, taking risks, and being willing to fail.

Be resilient: Modeling resilience in the face of setbacks or failures can help children learn to bounce back from adversity and develop a growth mindset. This means approaching challenges with a positive attitude and a willingness to learn from mistakes.

Show empathy: Modeling empathy and kindness can help children learn to value themselves and others. This means showing compassion, listening actively, and responding with kindness and understanding.

When modeling confident behavior, it's important to keep in mind that children learn through observation and experience.

Parents can set a positive example by practicing confident behaviors themselves, but they also need to provide opportunities for their children to practice and develop these skills on their own.

This can include encouraging children to take risks, providing positive feedback and encouragement, and offering support and guidance when needed.

By providing a safe and supportive environment, parents can help their children develop the confidence they need to succeed in all areas of their lives. In addition, parents should also be aware of the messages they are sending through their own behavior.

This means avoiding negative self-talk, being aware of body language, and refraining from comparing themselves or their children to others. By modeling confident behavior and positive self-image, parents can help their children develop a sense of self-worth and self-assurance that will serve them well throughout their lives.

In conclusion, modeling confident behavior is one of the most important things parents can do to help their children overcome shyness and develop confidence.

By being positive, practicing assertiveness, taking care of oneself, embracing challenges, practicing positive self-talk, being resilient, and showing empathy, parents can set a positive example for their children and help them develop the confidence they need to succeed in all areas of their lives.

Praise effort, not just achievement

Praising effort is a crucial aspect of developing confidence in children. When children are praised for their effort, they learn to value the process of learning and working hard, rather than just the end result. This type of praise can help children feel more confident in their abilities and motivated to continue learning and growing.

Here are some tips for praising effort, rather than just achievement:

Recognize the value of effort: Parents should help their children understand that effort is important, regardless of the outcome. Praising a child for their effort shows them that their hard work and dedication are appreciated, regardless of whether they succeed or fail.

Focus on the process: Instead of just praising the end result, parents should also praise the process that their child went through to achieve that result. For example, if a child worked hard on a project, parents could praise the time and effort they put into it, as well as the creative ideas they came up with.

Be specific: When praising effort, it's important to be specific about what exactly the child did well. This helps the child understand what they did right and reinforces the behavior they exhibited. For example, a parent might say "I'm so proud of how hard you worked on your homework. You really took your time and double-checked your answers, which shows how committed you are to doing well in school."

Avoid empty praise: Empty praise, or praise that is given without any real substance, can actually do more harm than good. Children can see through empty praise and may feel like they are being patronized. It's important to provide genuine praise that is based on specific achievements or behaviors.

Encourage perseverance: Praising effort can help children develop perseverance and a growth mindset. When children know that their hard work is valued, they are more likely to keep trying even in the face of challenges or setbacks. Parents can encourage this by praising their child's persistence and determination, even when things are difficult.

Foster intrinsic motivation: When children are praised for their effort, they develop a sense of intrinsic motivation. They learn to value the process of learning and working hard, rather than just the external rewards of success. This type of motivation can help children develop a lifelong love of learning and a sense of personal fulfillment.

Children also need to learn to cope with failure and setbacks, and praising effort alone may not provide the complete picture. Parents should also help their children understand that it's okay to fail sometimes, and that failure can be an important learning experience.

In addition, parents should be aware of the messages they are sending through their praise. Praising only for achievement can create a sense of pressure and anxiety in children, while praise for effort can help children feel more relaxed and motivated to learn.

Parents should avoid over-praising, which can lead to inflated egos and a sense of entitlement, and instead focus on providing genuine, specific praise that is based on the child's actual accomplishments. In conclusion, praising effort is an important part of developing confidence in children.

By recognizing the value of effort, focusing on the process, being specific, avoiding empty praise, encouraging perseverance, fostering intrinsic motivation, and avoiding comparisons, parents can help their children develop motivation that will serve them well throughout their lives.

When children know that their hard work and dedication are appreciated, they are more likely to continue working hard and trying their best, even in the face of challenges and setbacks. With the right kind of praise and encouragement, children can develop a growth mindset and a sense of self-worth that will stay with them for years to come.

Teach problem-solving skills

Problem-solving skills are a crucial part of a child's development. Children who learn how to solve problems are more confident, independent, and better equipped to deal with challenges in their lives. Teaching children problem-solving skills can also help them become more creative and innovative, as they learn how to approach problems from different angles and come up with new solutions.

Here are some tips for teaching problem-solving skills to children:

Encourage curiosity: Children who are curious about the world around them are more likely to ask questions and seek out solutions to problems. Encourage your child's curiosity by answering their questions, asking them questions in return, and providing them with opportunities to explore and learn.

Model problem-solving behavior: Children learn best by example, so make sure to model good problem-solving behavior. Show your child how to approach a problem, break it down into smaller parts, and come up with creative solutions. Explain your thinking process as you go along, so your child can see how you are reasoning things out.

Help children identify problems: Many children may not even realize that they are facing a problem. Help your child identify situations where a problem exists, and encourage them to think about different solutions. For example, if your child is having trouble making friends at school, help them identify the problem and brainstorm ways to solve it.

Teach problem-solving steps: Teach your child the basic steps of problem-solving, which include identifying the problem, brainstorming solutions, evaluating the options, choosing a solution, and implementing it. Practice these steps with your child, and help them apply them to real-life situations.

Encourage critical thinking: Critical thinking skills are an essential part of problem-solving. Encourage your child to think critically by asking open-ended questions that require them to think deeply and reflect on their ideas. For example, ask your child "Why do you think that happened?" or "What do you think would happen if we tried this instead?"

Practice problem-solving with fun activities: Engage your child in fun activities that require problem-solving, such as puzzles, board games, or building projects. These activities help children develop critical thinking skills and provide them with opportunities to practice problem-solving in a safe and supportive environment.

Teach decision-making skills: Decision-making is an important part of problem-solving. Teach your child how to weigh the pros and cons of different options, and how to make decisions based on their values and priorities. Encourage creativity: Encourage your child to think creatively when approaching a problem. Help them brainstorm unique solutions and consider alternative perspectives. Encourage them to think outside the box and come up with innovative solutions.

Encourage collaboration: Problem-solving often involves collaboration and teamwork. Encourage your child to work with others to solve problems and to listen to different perspectives. Teach them how to communicate effectively and to negotiate with others to find common ground.

Provide positive feedback: Provide positive feedback when your child successfully solves a problem. This reinforces their problem-solving skills and encourages them to continue using these skills in the future. Teaching problem-solving skills to children is a process that takes time and practice.

As parents, it's important to provide children with opportunities to practice problem-solving and to encourage them to think creatively and critically.

By teaching problem-solving skills, parents can help their children become more confident, independent, and innovative thinkers who are well-equipped to deal with the challenges that life may throw their way.

Focus on strengths

Focusing on strengths is an approach that involves recognizing and nurturing the positive qualities and skills that children possess. Instead of solely focusing on weaknesses or areas where children may struggle, this approach emphasizes building on existing strengths and encouraging children to use their unique talents and abilities to achieve success.

Here are some ways parents can focus on their child's strengths:

Identify strengths: Start by identifying your child's strengths. Take note of things they enjoy doing, excel in, or seem to have a natural talent for. For example, your child may have a talent for music, be a great athlete, or have a keen sense of empathy.

Encourage interests: Encourage your child to pursue their interests and hobbies. This can help them develop their strengths and build their self-esteem. Provide opportunities for them to practice their skills and explore new interests. For example, if your child enjoys playing soccer, sign them up for a local league or find opportunities for them to practice with friends.

Provide positive feedback: Provide positive feedback when your child displays their strengths. Let them know that you recognize and appreciate their talents and encourage them to continue using them. For example, if your child excels at drawing, compliment them on their artwork and encourage them to keep creating.

Set goals: Help your child set goals that align with their strengths. This can help them stay motivated and focused on using their strengths to achieve success. For example, if your child is interested in science, help them set a goal to participate in a science fair or enroll in a science-focused summer camp.

Provide opportunities for success: Provide your child with opportunities to use their strengths and succeed. This can help them build confidence and develop a sense of competence. For example, if your child is a great writer, encourage them to write stories or poems and share them with friends or family.

Celebrate successes: Celebrate your child's successes, both big and small. This reinforces their positive behavior and encourages them to continue using their strengths. For example, if your child receives a high grade on a project they worked hard on, celebrate their success with a special activity or treat.

Support weaknesses: While it's important to focus on strengths, it's also important to support weaknesses. Help your child identify areas where they may struggle and provide support and resources to help them improve. For example, if your child struggles with math, provide them with extra support, such as tutoring or online resources.

Foster a growth mindset: Encourage your child to embrace a growth mindset. This involves believing that abilities can be developed through hard work and dedication. Help your child understand that it's okay to make mistakes and that learning from them is a part of the growth process.

Model positive behavior: Model positive behavior by focusing on your own strengths and using them to achieve success. This can inspire your child to do the same and help them see the value in focusing on their own strengths.

Be patient: Remember that building on strengths is a process that takes time and patience. Encourage your child to practice and develop their strengths, but also be patient and allow them to grow at their own pace. Focusing on strengths is a positive approach that can help children develop confidence, self-esteem, and a sense of purpose.

By recognizing and nurturing their unique talents and abilities, parents can help their children reach their full potential and achieve success in all areas of life.

Practice positive self-talk

Positive self-talk is an essential tool that can help shy and lacking confidence children to build self-esteem, reduce anxiety, and improve overall mental health. The practice of positive self-talk involves using supportive and positive language to talk to oneself, shifting negative thoughts into constructive and encouraging ones.

Children who struggle with shyness and lack of confidence often face challenges in social situations, and may experience anxiety and stress that can affect their academic and personal development. Positive self-talk is a powerful way to help these children to overcome their fears, develop self-assurance, and achieve their full potential.

Here are some tips to help shy and lacking confidence children practice positive self-talk:

Identify negative self-talk: The first step in practicing positive self-talk is to help children identify negative self-talk patterns. This can involve teaching them to pay attention to their inner voice and the things they say to themselves. Encourage them to recognize when their thoughts are negative or self-critical and help them to challenge these thoughts and replace them with positive self-talk.

Use positive affirmations: Positive affirmations are positive statements that you can use to counteract negative self-talk. They can help you build confidence, increase self-esteem, and promote a positive outlook. When children are struggling with shyness and lack of confidence, positive affirmations can be a great way to help them overcome their negative self-talk. Encourage them to create their own positive affirmations that resonate with them and feel authentic. For example, "I am capable of making friends," "I am worthy of love and respect," and "I am brave and confident." These affirmations should be repeated regularly to reinforce positive self-talk and gradually shift negative thought patterns.

Use supportive language: Using supportive language when talking to children who struggle with shyness and lack of confidence is crucial. Children need to hear kind, compassionate, and gentle words to help them feel safe and secure. Encourage them to talk about their feelings and emotions, and provide them with validation and support. Use phrases like "I am here for you," "You can do this," and "I am proud of you" to show your support and help build their confidence.

Reframe negative thoughts: When children experience negative thoughts, it can be helpful to reframe them into more positive and constructive statements. This is a way to teach children how to challenge negative thoughts and transform them into positive ones. For example, if a child thinks "I am too shy to make friends," you can help them reframe this thought into "I am still learning how to make friends, but I am making progress." This helps them develop a growth mindset and encourages them to keep trying.

Visualize success: Visualizing success can be a powerful tool for children struggling with shyness and lack of confidence. Encourage them to imagine themselves succeeding and achieving their goals. Help them picture themselves making new friends, participating in social activities, or speaking up in class. Visualization helps children stay motivated and focused on their goals, and it can boost their confidence and self-esteem.

Practice gratitude: Gratitude is an essential element of positive self-talk. Encourage children to take time to appreciate the good things in their lives and focus on what they have, rather than what they lack. Help them identify the things they are grateful for and use positive self-talk to reinforce the belief that they are blessed and that good things are coming their way.

Stay present: Staying present and focusing on the moment is another way to help children who struggle with shyness and lack of confidence. Teach them to use positive self-talk to keep themselves grounded and centered in the present moment. Help them understand that they can handle whatever comes their way, and that they have the strength and resilience to overcome any challenges.

Practice self-care: Self-care is an important part of practicing positive self-talk. Encourage children to take care of themselves physically, emotionally, and mentally. Teach them the importance of exercise, healthy eating, getting enough sleep, and stress-reducing activities like yoga or meditation. Self-care helps children feel good about themselves and reinforces positive self-talk.

Surround yourself with positivity: Surrounding yourself with positive people and positive environments is crucial for building confidence and overcoming shyness. Encourage children to seek out positive relationships and experiences, and to avoid negative people and situations that can bring them down. Help them use positive self-talk to reinforce the belief that they are worthy of positive experiences and relationships.

Be patient and persistent: Finally, be patient and persistent when helping children practice positive self-talk. It takes time and practice to develop this skill, so don't give up if you don't see immediate results. Keep practicing, and eventually, positive self-talk will become a natural part of their thinking process.

In conclusion, positive self-talk is a powerful tool for building self-confidence, reducing anxiety, and improving overall mental health, particularly in shy and lacking confidence children. By identifying negative self-talk patterns, using positive affirmations, supportive language, visualizing success, and practicing self-care, children can learn to shift negative thoughts to more constructive and encouraging ones.

It's also essential to surround yourself with positivity, be patient and persistent, and seek support from trusted friends, family members, or professionals when needed. With consistent practice, children can cultivate a positive and empowering inner dialogue that will serve them well throughout their lives.

Set achievable goals

Setting achievable goals is an essential part of building confidence, motivation, and self-esteem in shy children. When children set achievable goals, they are more likely to succeed, which can boost their confidence and give them a sense of accomplishment.

Moreover, the skills they learn from setting and achieving goals can help them in other areas of their lives. In this chapter, we will explore the different ways to help shy children set achievable goals and build their confidence.

Start with a Clear Vision: The first step in setting achievable goals is to have a clear vision of what you want to achieve. It's essential to help children define their goals in specific, measurable terms, and be clear about what they want to accomplish. Having a clear vision will help them stay focused and motivated as they work towards their goals.

For instance, if a child wants to make new friends, you can help them define their goal in specific terms. For example, "I want to make one new friend by the end of the month" is a specific and measurable goal.

It's easier to focus on one friend than to try and make several friends at once. Moreover, it's essential to make sure that the goal is achievable for the child's age and personality.

Break Goals Down into Smaller Steps: Big goals can be overwhelming and hard to achieve. Breaking them down into smaller, more manageable steps can make them less daunting and help children make progress towards their goals.

For example, if a child's goal is to speak up more in class, you can help them break it down into smaller steps, such as answering one question in class each day or asking the teacher for help with a problem.

Breaking the goal into smaller steps helps to make the goal less intimidating, and achieving each small step can be a source of motivation for the child. When they complete a step, they will feel a sense of accomplishment, which can boost their confidence and help them to continue working towards their goal.

Big goals can be overwhelming and hard to achieve, especially for shy children who may lack self-confidence and motivation.

Breaking goals down into smaller, more manageable steps can make them less daunting and help shy children make progress towards their goals. For example, if a shy child's goal is to create a series of drawings that tell a story, they may break it down into smaller goals such as:

1. Choose a theme for the story
2. Sketch rough drafts of each drawing
3. Select a color palette
4. Create final drawings
5. Create a storyboard

6. Put the drawings in order
7. Share the finished product with family and friends

Make Goals Realistic: Goals should be realistic and achievable, based on the child's current skills, resources, and circumstances. Setting unrealistic goals can lead to frustration, disappointment, and a lack of motivation.

Be honest with the child about what they can realistically achieve, and set goals that challenge them but are still within reach.

For instance, if a child has never played an instrument before, it might be unrealistic to expect them to become a professional musician in a year. Instead, setting a goal to learn to play a simple song on an instrument is more achievable.

Set Deadlines: Deadlines can help children stay motivated and focused on their goals. Setting realistic deadlines for each step of their goal, and making sure they are achievable, can help them measure progress, hold themselves accountable, and celebrate milestones along the way.

For example, if a child wants to learn a new language, setting a goal to learn 10 new words each week and have a basic conversation in three months can help them stay motivated.

Create a Plan: Once children have set their goals, it's essential to help them create a plan to achieve them. Breaking their goals down into smaller steps and creating a timeline and action plan to help them achieve each step is important.

Identify any obstacles or challenges that may arise, and come up with strategies to overcome them. A plan helps them to focus on what needs to be done to achieve their goals, and it also helps to keep them on track.

Monitor Progress: Regularly monitoring progress towards goals is important. Tracking progress, celebrating milestones, and making adjustments as needed can help children stay motivated, identify areas for improvement, and make adjustments to their plan if necessary.

For instance, if a child's goal is to read a book by the end of the month, tracking their progress and celebrating milestones such as completing each chapter can help them stay motivated.

One of the essential steps in goal-setting is to celebrate achievements along the way. This can be anything from reaching a small milestone to completing a more significant task. Celebrating these accomplishments can help shy children stay motivated and reinforce their belief in themselves.

It's essential to reward yourself or your child when they achieve a goal or milestone, even if it's something as small as finishing a homework assignment. It helps to use positive self-talk to reinforce the belief that they are capable of achieving their goals.

Another critical aspect of setting achievable goals is being willing to adjust them as needed. Life can be unpredictable, and circumstances may change.

Being open to adjusting goals and plans if necessary can help children avoid becoming discouraged by setbacks or obstacles. It's crucial to remember that setbacks are a natural part of the goal-setting process, and they can be opportunities for growth and learning.

Step 1: Get Support

The first step in setting achievable goals for shy children is to get support. Children who are shy often struggle to speak up for themselves and may be reluctant to ask for help.

As a parent or caregiver, it is important to create a safe and supportive environment where the child feels comfortable sharing their thoughts and feelings.

This can be achieved by:
Active Listening: Listening to what the child is saying, acknowledging their feelings, and validating their experiences. Encourage them to express their thoughts and feelings and respond with empathy and understanding.

Encouragement: Offering encouragement and support for their efforts. Praise their achievements, no matter how small, and show them that their efforts are valued.

Role Model: As an adult or caregiver, you can model positive behavior by setting your own achievable goals and demonstrating persistence in achieving them. This can help the child to see that it is possible to overcome obstacles and achieve their goals.

Step 2: Keep a Positive Attitude

The second step in setting achievable goals for shy children is to keep a positive attitude. Children who are shy may struggle with self-doubt and negative self-talk. Encouraging positive self-talk can help to build confidence and self-esteem.

Here are a few ways to encourage a positive attitude:

Affirmations: Encourage the child to say positive affirmations to themselves each day. This can be as simple as saying "I am capable" or "I can do this."

Visualization: Ask the child to visualize themselves achieving their goals. This can help to build confidence and motivation.

Positive Reinforcement: Focus on the positive rather than the negative. Celebrate the child's successes and offer constructive feedback for areas that need improvement.

Measuring Progress: Once goals have been set, it's important to measure progress regularly. This not only helps the child see how far they have come, but it can also help them stay motivated and focused on their goal. One way to measure progress is to break the goal down into smaller, more manageable steps.

For example, if the goal is to learn a new song on an instrument, the child could break it down into steps such as learning the melody, practicing the chords, and playing the entire song from memory.

Another way to measure progress is to keep a journal or chart. This can be a fun and visual way for the child to see how far they have come and what they still need to work on. For example, they could create a chart with different milestones or steps to reach their goal, and mark off each one as they complete it.

Seeking Feedback: Seeking feedback is another important part of setting achievable goals. Feedback can help the child understand what they are doing well and what they need to work on. It can also provide encouragement and support, which can be especially important for shy children who may be hesitant to take risks.

One way to seek feedback is to ask a trusted friend or family member for their thoughts on the child's progress. This can be a great way to get an outside perspective and see where the child may need to focus their efforts. Another option is to seek feedback from a teacher or mentor. These individuals can provide valuable insights and guidance on how to achieve the child's goals.

Being Persistent: Finally, it's important to be persistent when setting achievable goals. Achieving a goal takes time and effort, and there may be setbacks and obstacles along the way. It's important to encourage the child to stay focused and determined, even when things get tough.

One way to help the child stay persistent is to remind them of their progress and achievements along the way. Celebrating small victories can help boost their confidence and keep them motivated to continue working towards their goal.

Additionally, it's important to remind them that setbacks and mistakes are a natural part of the learning process, and that they can use these experiences to grow and improve.

In conclusion, setting achievable goals is a critical skill for shy children to learn. By setting goals that are challenging but achievable, measuring progress, seeking feedback, and being persistent, children can build confidence and develop the skills they need to succeed. With the right support and encouragement, shy children can learn to overcome their fears and achieve their goals.

Celebrate success

Celebrating success is an important part of building confidence in shy children. It reinforces progress, builds self-esteem, and motivates them to keep working towards their goals.

When shy children achieve their goals, they may feel hesitant to celebrate or acknowledge their success. Therefore, it is important to teach them how to celebrate success in a way that is comfortable for them.

Here are some effective ways to celebrate success:

Reflect on the achievement: After achieving a goal, take a moment to reflect on what has been accomplished. Think about the hard work, dedication, and effort that went into achieving the goal. This can help build a sense of pride and confidence in oneself.

Encourage shy children to write down their accomplishments, which can serve as a reminder of their success in the future.

Plan a special activity: Plan a special activity to celebrate the success. It can be something as simple as going for a walk, having a picnic, or playing a game.

The important thing is to do something that brings joy and celebrates the achievement. It is important to let the child choose the activity, as they know what they enjoy the most. Share the success with others: Sharing success with others can be a great way to build confidence and reinforce progress.

Encourage shy children to share their success with family, friends, or a trusted teacher. Talking about their achievement can help build confidence and reinforce the progress they have made. The important thing is to choose something that the child will truly enjoy.

Hold a ceremony: Holding a small ceremony to acknowledge the achievement can be a great way to build a sense of accomplishment and pride.

It could be as simple as lighting a candle or saying a few words. The important thing is to acknowledge the hard work and dedication that went into achieving the goal.

Take a break:
Taking a break and relaxing is important after achieving a goal. It can be exhausting, and it is important to take time to recharge and refocus.

Encourage shy children to take a break and do something relaxing, such as reading a book, listening to music, or taking a bath. In conclusion, celebrating success is an important part of building confidence in shy children. It reinforces progress, builds self-esteem, and motivates them to keep working towards their goals.

Encouraging shy children to celebrate their successes in a way that is comfortable for them can help build their confidence and improve their self-esteem.

Achieving a goal is a significant accomplishment, and it is essential to celebrate successes, no matter how big or small they are.

Celebrating success is not just about having a good time; it is a way to acknowledge and reinforce progress, build confidence, and maintain motivation towards future goals.

Avoid labeling your child as "shy"

Shyness is a natural personality trait that some children possess, but it does not define their entire being. By labeling a child as "shy," it can create a self-fulfilling prophecy that can limit their opportunities and prevent them from reaching their full potential.

Here are some reasons why labeling a child as "shy" can be detrimental:

It can reinforce negative self-perceptions: Labeling a child as "shy" can reinforce negative self-perceptions and create a self-fulfilling prophecy. Children who are labeled as "shy" may begin to see themselves as socially incompetent and avoid social situations altogether.

It can limit opportunities: Labeling a child as "shy" can limit their opportunities for social interaction, which can hinder their social and emotional development. Children who are labeled as "shy" may be less likely to participate in social activities or engage with their peers, which can lead to feelings of isolation and loneliness.

It can lead to stigma and stereotypes: Labeling a child as "shy" can lead to stigma and stereotypes that can negatively impact their self-esteem and social relationships. Children who are labeled as "shy" may be viewed as socially awkward or timid, which can make it difficult for them to form meaningful relationships with their peers.

It can create unnecessary pressure: Labeling a child as "shy" can create unnecessary pressure for them to change their personality. Children who are labeled as "shy" may feel like they have to become more outgoing or sociable, which can be stressful and overwhelming.

So, what can parents do instead of labeling their child as "shy"?

Here are some strategies to consider:

Acknowledge their strengths: Instead of focusing on their shyness, acknowledge your child's strengths and positive qualities. Help them to recognize their unique talents and abilities, and encourage them to pursue their interests and passions.

Provide support and encouragement: Provide your child with support and encouragement to help them overcome their shyness. Offer praise and positive feedback for their efforts, and provide gentle guidance and support when they need it.

Avoid pushing them out of their comfort zone: While it's important to encourage your child to try new things, it's also important to respect their boundaries and avoid pushing them out of their comfort zone. Instead, encourage them to take small steps towards overcoming their shyness, and provide them with support and encouragement along the way.

Encourage social interactions: Encourage your child to engage in social activities and interact with their peers. Provide them with opportunities to participate in group activities, such as sports or clubs, and encourage them to invite friends over for playdates or outings.

Focus on building social skills: Instead of labeling your child as "shy," focus on building their social skills. Help them to develop social skills such as active listening, empathy, and communication, and provide them with opportunities to practice these skills in real-life situations.

In conclusion, labeling a child as "shy" can have negative consequences on their self-esteem, social development, and overall well-being. Instead of focusing on their shyness, parents can acknowledge their strengths, provide support and encouragement, avoid pushing them out of their comfort zone, encourage social interactions, and focus on building their social skills.

By implementing these strategies, parents can help their child to overcome their shyness and reach their full potential without limiting their opportunities or reinforcing negative self-perceptions.

Offer encouragement and support

Encouragement and support are essential for children's development, self-esteem, and overall well-being. When children receive encouragement and support, they are more likely to feel confident, motivated, and capable of achieving their goals. Additionally, encouragement and support can help children build resilience, cope with challenges, and develop a positive sense of self.

Here are some strategies parents can use to offer encouragement and support to their children:

Offer specific and genuine praise: When children receive specific and genuine praise, they feel seen, heard, and appreciated. Rather than using general praise like "good job," parents can offer specific praise that acknowledges their child's effort and progress. For example, "I'm proud of how hard you worked on that project" or "I noticed how much you've improved in math."

Listen actively: When parents listen actively to their children, they demonstrate that they value their opinions and perspectives. Active listening involves giving children your full attention, asking open-ended questions, and reflecting back what you heard. This can help children feel heard and validated, which can build their self-esteem and sense of worth.

Provide positive feedback: Providing positive feedback can help children feel encouraged and motivated to continue their efforts. Parents can provide positive feedback by highlighting their child's strengths, acknowledging their progress, and offering suggestions for improvement. This can help children feel more confident and capable of achieving their goals.

Set realistic expectations: Setting realistic expectations can help children feel motivated and encouraged to achieve their goals. When expectations are too high or unrealistic, children may feel overwhelmed, anxious, or discouraged. By setting goals that are challenging but achievable, parents can help children build their confidence and self-efficacy.

Encourage independence: Encouraging independence can help children build their self-esteem and sense of autonomy. Parents can encourage independence by allowing their children to make choices, take on responsibilities, and solve problems on their own. This can help children feel capable and competent, which can build their self-esteem and motivation.

Provide emotional support: Providing emotional support can help children feel validated and supported during challenging times. Parents can provide emotional support by offering comfort, empathy, and understanding. Additionally, parents can help children develop coping skills and problem-solving strategies to help them manage their emotions and navigate difficult situations.

Celebrate successes: Celebrating successes can help children feel proud of their achievements and motivated to continue their efforts. Parents can celebrate successes by offering praise, recognition, and rewards. Additionally, parents can help children set new goals and encourage them to continue to strive for their personal best.

Focus on effort, not just outcomes: Focusing on effort can help children feel valued and appreciated for their hard work and perseverance. Parents can focus on effort by acknowledging their child's progress, highlighting their strengths, and providing positive feedback. This can help children feel motivated and encouraged to continue their efforts, even when faced with challenges.

Be available and responsive: Being available and responsive can help children feel supported and secure. Parents can be available by setting aside dedicated time to spend with their children, responding to their needs promptly, and being present and engaged when they are together. This can help children feel valued and loved, which can build their self-esteem and sense of belonging.

Be a positive role model: Being a positive role model can help children learn healthy habits and behaviors. Parents can be positive role models by modeling positive attitudes, behaviors, and coping skills.

Additionally, parents can demonstrate healthy communication and problem-solving skills, which can help children learn how to navigate social relationships and manage conflicts effectively.

In conclusion, offering encouragement and support to children is essential for their development, self-esteem, and overall well-being.

By offering specific and genuine praise, listening actively, providing positive feedback, setting realistic expectations, providing emotional support, celebrating successes, focusing on effort, being available and responsive, and being a positive role model, parents can help their children feel confident, capable, and motivated to achieve their goals.

When children feel supported and encouraged, they are more likely to take risks, try new things, and develop a positive sense of self.

Additionally, children who receive encouragement and support are more likely to develop healthy coping skills, manage stress and anxiety, and build strong social relationships. It is important to note that offering encouragement and support does not mean shielding children from challenges or difficulties.

Rather, it means providing a safe and supportive environment where children feel empowered to take on challenges, learn from their mistakes, and grow and develop as individuals. Parents can help their children build resilience by teaching them problem-solving skills, encouraging them to learn from their failures, and helping them develop a growth mindset.

By focusing on effort and progress rather than just outcomes, parents can help their children develop a sense of resilience and perseverance that will serve them well throughout their lives.

In conclusion, offering encouragement and support to children is one of the most important things parents can do to promote their children's development, self-esteem, and well-being.

By offering specific and genuine praise, listening actively, providing positive feedback, setting realistic expectations, encouraging independence, providing emotional support, celebrating successes, focusing on effort, being available and responsive, and being a positive role model, parents can help their children build the confidence, motivation, and resilience they need to succeed in life.

Teach assertiveness skills

Assertiveness is the ability to express oneself in a clear and confident manner while respecting the rights and opinions of others. **Assertiveness skills are important** because they allow individuals to effectively communicate their needs, desires, and boundaries, and can help them navigate social situations with confidence and self-assurance.

Children who lack assertiveness skills may struggle to advocate for themselves, express their opinions, or establish healthy boundaries in relationships. They may also be more vulnerable to peer pressure, bullying, or other negative social interactions.

Fortunately, assertiveness skills can be taught and developed over time.
Here are some tips for parents to help their children learn and practice assertiveness:

Teach communication skills: Effective communication is the foundation of assertiveness. Teach your child how to express themselves clearly and respectfully, using "I" statements to communicate their needs and feelings.

Encourage self-awareness: Help your child become aware of their own needs, feelings, and boundaries. Encourage them to reflect on their values and beliefs, and to develop a sense of self-worth and self-respect.

Role-play different scenarios: Practice assertiveness skills by role-playing different scenarios with your child. For example, you could role-play asking for help, saying "no" to a request, or expressing a disagreement.

Set expectations: Make it clear to your child that you expect them to communicate their needs and feelings assertively, and that you will support them in doing so.

Model assertive behavior: Children learn by example, so be a positive role model for your child by demonstrating assertive behavior in your own interactions. Use "I" statements to express your needs and feelings, and respect the boundaries and opinions of others.

Encourage problem-solving: Help your child develop problem-solving skills so they can assertively address conflicts and issues as they arise. Encourage them to brainstorm solutions and consider the perspective of others.

Provide positive reinforcement: When your child demonstrates assertive behavior, provide positive reinforcement by acknowledging their efforts and praising their success.

Address fear and anxiety: Fear and anxiety can make it difficult for children to be assertive. Encourage your child to talk about their fears and anxieties, and help them develop coping strategies to manage these emotions.

Teach resilience:

Building resilience can help your child bounce back from rejection, disappointment, or negative feedback. Teach your child that it's okay to make mistakes, and encourage them to view challenges as opportunities for growth and learning.

Encouraging risk-taking in safe environments

Encouraging risk-taking in safe environments is an important part of helping children develop confidence and resilience. When children take risks and experience success, they build self-esteem and develop a sense of mastery over their environment. On the other hand, when they experience failure, they learn important lessons about perseverance, problem-solving, and resilience.

However, it is important to create a safe and supportive environment for children to take risks. This means setting clear boundaries and expectations, providing support and encouragement, and ensuring that the risks are age-appropriate and manageable.

Here are some tips for parents to encourage safe risk-taking:

Create a supportive environment: Children are more likely to take risks when they feel safe and supported. Make sure your child knows that you are there to support them and provide guidance, and that you will be proud of them no matter what the outcome.

Set clear boundaries: While it's important to encourage risk-taking, it's also important to set clear boundaries to ensure that the risks are safe and age-appropriate. Make sure your child understands what is and is not allowed, and provide guidance as needed.

Start small: Encourage your child to take small risks at first, such as trying a new food or activity. As they become more comfortable with risk-taking, they may be more willing to take on bigger challenges.

Encourage problem-solving: When your child takes risks, encourage them to problem-solve and think critically about the situation. This will help them develop important skills for managing risk and uncertainty.

Emphasize effort over outcome: When your child takes risks, focus on their effort rather than the outcome. This will help them develop a growth mindset and a sense of resilience in the face of failure.

Provide positive reinforcement: When your child takes a risk and experiences success, provide positive reinforcement by praising their efforts and acknowledging their achievement. Encourage exploration: Encourage your child to explore their environment and try new things. This will help them build confidence and develop a sense of curiosity and adventure.

Allow for natural consequences: When your child takes a risk and experiences failure, allow for natural consequences to occur. This will help them learn important lessons about decision-making and problem-solving.

Be a positive role model: Children learn by example, so be a positive role model for risk-taking by trying new things and taking on challenges yourself.

Encouraging safe risk-taking can be a great way to help children develop confidence, resilience, and a sense of mastery over their environment.

By providing support and guidance, setting clear boundaries, and emphasizing effort over outcome, parents can help their children learn important lessons about decision-making, problem-solving, and resilience.

Help your child manage anxiety

Anxiety is a common experience for children, particularly as they face new challenges and transitions. While some anxiety is normal and even healthy, it can become a problem when it interferes with daily functioning or causes distress. As a parent, there are many ways you can help your child manage anxiety and develop coping strategies.

Here are some tips for helping your child manage anxiety:

Validate their feelings: It is important to acknowledge your child's feelings and let them know that anxiety is a normal experience. Let them know that it is okay to feel anxious, and that you are there to support them.

Provide a safe and supportive environment: Creating a safe and supportive environment can help reduce anxiety. Make sure your child feels comfortable talking to you about their fears and worries, and that they know you will listen and provide support.

Teach relaxation techniques: Relaxation techniques, such as deep breathing or progressive muscle relaxation, can be effective in reducing anxiety. Help your child learn these techniques and practice them regularly.

Encourage physical activity: Exercise is a natural stress-reliever and can help reduce anxiety. Encourage your child to engage in physical activity, whether it be a team sport or an individual activity such as yoga or running.

Provide healthy nutrition: A healthy diet can have a positive impact on mood and reduce anxiety. Encourage your child to eat a balanced diet with plenty of fruits, vegetables, and whole grains.

Develop a routine: A consistent routine can help reduce anxiety by providing a sense of structure and predictability. Create a daily routine with your child that includes time for relaxation and physical activity.

Address the source of anxiety: Try to identify the source of your child's anxiety and address it directly. Whether it be a specific fear or worry, working to address the source of anxiety can be effective in reducing symptoms.

Practice mindfulness: Mindfulness techniques, such as meditation or yoga, can help reduce anxiety by promoting a sense of calm and relaxation. Encourage your child to practice mindfulness regularly.

Seek professional help: If your child's anxiety is severe or interfering with daily functioning, seek professional help from a mental health professional or counselor. They can provide additional support and guidance.

Managing anxiety can be a challenging experience for children and parents alike. However, with the right strategies and support, it is possible to help your child develop effective coping strategies and reduce anxiety.

By providing a safe and supportive environment, teaching relaxation techniques, encouraging physical activity and healthy nutrition, addressing the source of anxiety, promoting positive self-talk and mindfulness, and seeking professional help if necessary, parents can help their child manage anxiety and develop resilience.

Encourage self-expression through art or writing

Self-expression is a vital part of a child's emotional and psychological development. Encouraging self-expression through art or writing can help children to develop a deeper understanding of themselves and their feelings, and can provide a healthy outlet for their emotions.

Here are some ways that parents can encourage their children to express themselves through art or writing:

Provide a variety of materials: Providing a range of materials for your child to use can help them to express themselves more freely. Consider stocking up on paper, markers, paint, colored pencils, and other materials that your child enjoys using.

Give your child the time and space to create: Set aside dedicated time for your child to create, and create a space where they can work without distractions. This can help them to focus and be more productive.

Encourage experimentation: Encourage your child to experiment with different materials and techniques, and to try new things. This can help them to discover new ways of expressing themselves and build their confidence.

Provide prompts or themes: Providing prompts or themes can help your child to get started and give them a sense of direction. For example, you could suggest that they create a drawing or story about a favorite memory or something that makes them happy.

Validate your child's work: When your child shares their art or writing with you, take the time to show interest and ask questions about what they have created. This can help to validate their efforts and encourage them to continue expressing themselves.

Create together: Creating art or writing together can be a fun and rewarding activity for both you and your child. You can collaborate on a project or each work on your own creations side by side.

Display their work: Displaying your child's artwork or writing can help to reinforce their sense of pride and accomplishment. Consider framing their work or hanging it up on the fridge or a bulletin board.

Keep a journal together: Keeping a journal together can provide a space for both you and your child to express yourselves and reflect on your thoughts and feelings. You can write about your day or use prompts to explore different topics.

Encourage your child to share their work with others: Encouraging your child to share their art or writing with others can help to build their confidence and provide them with valuable feedback.

You could suggest that they show their work to friends or family members, or even enter it into a local art or writing competition.

By encouraging self-expression through art or writing, parents can help their children to develop a deeper understanding of themselves and their feelings, and to build their confidence and self-esteem.

Whether it be through providing a variety of materials, encouraging experimentation, providing prompts, creating together, displaying their work, keeping a journal, or focusing on the process, there are many ways that parents can support their child's self-expression.

Celebrate diversity and difference

Shyness and low confidence in children can hinder their ability to learn and grow. As parents and educators, it is essential to create an environment that promotes confidence, self-esteem, and social skills in children. One way to achieve this is by celebrating diversity and differences among children.

We will explore the importance of celebrating diversity in combating shyness and low confidence in children.

What is Diversity?

Diversity refers to the variety of differences that exist among people. These differences can be seen in race, ethnicity, gender, religion, culture, language, and abilities.

Celebrating diversity means recognizing and valuing these differences and understanding that they make us unique and special.

Why is Celebrating Diversity Important?

Celebrating diversity is important because it promotes inclusivity, acceptance, and respect among people.

When children are exposed to diverse cultures and lifestyles, they develop a broader perspective of the world and learn to appreciate and respect differences. This can help reduce prejudice, discrimination, and bias in children and encourage them to embrace diversity.

How Does Celebrating Diversity Combat Shyness and Low Confidence in Children?

Celebrating diversity can combat shyness and low confidence in children in several ways:

Builds Confidence: When children are exposed to different cultures, languages, and lifestyles, they gain a better understanding of themselves and others. This can help them develop a sense of identity and confidence in who they are. They also learn to appreciate and accept their differences, which can boost their self-esteem.

Encourages Social Interaction: Celebrating diversity promotes social interaction among children. When children are exposed to diverse cultures and lifestyles, they are more likely to engage with others and learn to communicate and interact with people from different backgrounds. This can help combat shyness and social anxiety in children and improve their social skills.

Promotes Empathy: Celebrating diversity can help children develop empathy for others. When children learn about different cultures and lifestyles, they develop a better understanding of the challenges and experiences of others. This can help them become more compassionate and caring towards others, which can improve their social skills and combat shyness.

Reduces Prejudice and Discrimination: Celebrating diversity can help reduce prejudice and discrimination in children. When children are exposed to diverse cultures and lifestyles, they learn to appreciate and respect differences. This can help reduce bias and prejudice towards others and promote a more inclusive and accepting environment.

How to Celebrate Diversity in Children?

There are several ways to celebrate diversity in children:

Expose Children to Different Cultures: Exposing children to different cultures is a great way to celebrate diversity. This can be done by reading books, watching movies, and exploring different cuisines and traditions. It is also helpful to invite people from different cultures to share their experiences and traditions with children.

Encourage Diversity in Education: Encouraging diversity in education is essential. This can be done by incorporating diverse perspectives and cultures into the curriculum and ensuring that materials and resources reflect a diverse range of experiences.

Create a Safe and Inclusive Environment: Creating a safe and inclusive environment is crucial in celebrating diversity. This can be done by promoting respect, empathy, and inclusivity among children. It is also important to address any incidents of bias, discrimination, or bullying and provide support to those affected.

Use Positive Language: Using positive language is important when celebrating diversity. This means avoiding stereotypes, derogatory language, and negative assumptions. Instead, use language that promotes inclusivity, acceptance, and respect for differences. Conclusion

In conclusion, celebrating diversity is crucial in combating shyness and low confidence in children. By promoting inclusivity, acceptance, and respect for differences, children can develop a sense of identity and confidence in who they are.

Avoid comparing
your child to others

As parents, we often want our children to be the best version of themselves. However, in our pursuit of helping our children achieve their potential, we sometimes fall into the trap of comparing them to others. While it is natural to make comparisons, it can be harmful to our children's self-esteem and confidence.

We will explore the negative effects of comparing children to others and why it is important to avoid doing so.

Why Do Parents Compare Their Children to Others?

Parents may compare their children to others for various reasons. Some of the common reasons include:

Social Pressure: Parents may feel social pressure to ensure that their children meet certain standards or expectations. This pressure may come from other parents, family members, or society in general.

Fear of Failure: Parents may fear that their children will not succeed if they do not meet certain standards or expectations. They may compare their children to others to motivate them to work harder and achieve success.

Lack of Confidence: Parents may lack confidence in their parenting skills or their child's abilities. They may compare their children to others to ensure that they are doing the right things and to seek validation.

Negative Effects of Comparing Children to Others
Comparing children to others can have several
negative effects, including:

Low Self-Esteem: Comparing children to others can
lower their self-esteem and confidence. Children may
feel that they are not good enough or that they do not
measure up to others. This can lead to feelings of
inadequacy and self-doubt.

Resentment: Children may feel resentful towards the
person they are being compared to, especially if it is a
sibling or a friend. They may also feel resentful
towards the parent who is making the comparison.

Unhealthy Competition: Comparing children to
others can create an unhealthy sense of competition.
Children may feel that they need to compete with
others to gain approval or recognition from their
parents. This can lead to a constant need to compare
themselves to others and to feel that they are always
falling short.

Anxiety and Stress: Comparing children to others can
create feelings of anxiety and stress. Children may feel
that they need to constantly perform at a high level to
meet their parent's expectations. This can lead to
feelings of pressure and stress, which can affect their
mental health and well-being.

How to Avoid Comparing Your Child to Others?

Avoiding comparisons can be challenging, especially
if we have been conditioned to make them.

However, there are several strategies that parents can use to avoid making comparisons and promote a healthy sense of self-esteem and confidence in their children.

Focus on Your Child's Strengths: Instead of comparing your child to others, focus on their strengths and accomplishments. Celebrate their achievements and encourage them to pursue their interests and passions.

Avoid Negative Language: Avoid using negative language when talking to your child. Instead of saying "Why can't you be more like your sister?" say "You have your own unique strengths and abilities."

Set Realistic Expectations: Set realistic expectations for your child based on their abilities and interests. Avoid setting unrealistic expectations that may be difficult for your child to meet.

Encourage Individuality: Encourage your child to embrace their individuality and celebrate their unique qualities. Teach them that everyone has their own strengths and weaknesses and that it is okay to be different.

Be Mindful of Social Media: Social media can be a breeding ground for comparisons. Be mindful of the images and messages that your child is exposed to on social media and teach them to appreciate their own unique qualities.

Practice Self-Acceptance: As a parent, it is important to practice self-acceptance and avoid making comparisons to other parents or families. Lead by example and show your child that you are happy with who you are and that you value your own unique qualities.

Encourage Positive Self-Talk: Encourage your child to engage in positive self-talk. Teach them to focus on their strengths and accomplishments and to avoid negative self-talk that can lead to feelings of inadequacy and self-doubt.

Emphasize Effort Over Outcome: Emphasize the importance of effort over outcome. Teach your child that it is important to try their best and to focus on the process of learning and growing, rather than just the end result.

Teach Empathy: Teach your child to be empathetic towards others and to avoid making comparisons. Help them understand that everyone has their own unique qualities and that it is important to celebrate diversity and individuality.

Seek Professional Help: If you find that you are struggling with avoiding comparisons or that your child's self-esteem is suffering, seek professional help.

A therapist or counselor can help you and your child work through any issues and develop healthy coping strategies. Conclusion Comparing children to others can have negative effects on their self-esteem and confidence.

As parents, it is important to avoid making comparisons and to promote a healthy sense of individuality and self-acceptance in our children.

By focusing on our child's strengths, setting realistic expectations, and encouraging positive self-talk, we can help our children develop a strong sense of self-worth and confidence that will serve them well throughout their lives.

Foster a sense of independence

As children grow and develop, it is important for them to develop a sense of independence. Independence allows children to develop self-confidence, problem-solving skills, and decision-making abilities.

However, fostering a sense of independence in children can be challenging, especially in a society that places a lot of emphasis on conformity and following rules.

We will explore the importance of fostering a sense of independence in children and provide some strategies for parents to help their children develop this important trait.

Why Is Independence Important?

Builds Confidence: Independence helps children build self-confidence. When children are given the freedom to make their own decisions, they learn to trust their abilities and develop a sense of self-efficacy.

Encourages Critical Thinking: When children are allowed to make decisions for themselves, they are forced to think critically about the choices they make. This helps them develop problem-solving skills and encourages them to consider all possible outcomes before making a decision.

Teaches Responsibility: When children are given independence, they learn to take responsibility for their actions. This helps them develop a sense of accountability and encourages them to take ownership of their mistakes.

Enhances Creativity: Independence allows children to explore their interests and develop their creativity. This can lead to a greater sense of fulfillment and a stronger sense of identity.

Prepares for Adulthood: Ultimately, independence prepares children for adulthood. When children learn to be self-sufficient and make decisions for themselves, they are better equipped to navigate the challenges of adulthood.

Strategies for Fostering Independence in Children

Start Early: It is important to start fostering independence in children at an early age. This can be as simple as allowing children to choose their own clothes or decide what they want to eat for breakfast. Encourage Problem-Solving:

Encourage children to solve problems on their own. When faced with a challenge, ask them what they think they should do and guide them through the decision-making process.

Assign Age-Appropriate Chores: Giving children age-appropriate chores helps them develop a sense of responsibility and accountability. Chores can include tasks like making their bed, cleaning up their toys, or helping with laundry.

Allow for Risk-Taking: Allow children to take risks and make mistakes. This helps them learn from their experiences and develop a sense of resilience.

Encourage Open Communication: Encourage children to express their thoughts and feelings openly. This helps them develop communication skills and learn to advocate for themselves.

Allow for Choice: Give children choices whenever possible. This can be as simple as allowing them to choose what they want to wear or what activity they want to do after school.

Avoid Overprotecting: Overprotecting children can hinder their development of independence. It is important to strike a balance between keeping children safe and allowing them to explore the world on their own.

Praise Effort: When children take initiative or make decisions on their own, praise their efforts.

Lead by example: This can be as simple as talking aloud about your own decision-making process or involving your children in your own problem-solving. Conclusion Fostering a sense of independence in children is crucial for their overall development and prepares them for adulthood.

By providing opportunities for decision-making, encouraging problem-solving, and allowing for risk-taking, parents can help their children develop self-confidence, responsibility, and critical thinking skills. It is important to remember to provide g

uidance and support while avoiding overprotection. With these strategies, parents can help their children develop a strong sense of independence that will serve them well throughout their lives.

Seek professional help if needed

As parents, we want to do everything we can to support our children's growth and development. However, there are times when our best efforts are not enough and our children may need professional help. This can be a difficult decision to make, but seeking professional help can be a crucial step in helping our children overcome challenges and thrive.

We will discuss why it is important to seek professional help when needed and provide some guidance on how to do so.

Why Seek Professional Help?

Specialized Expertise: Professionals, such as psychologists and counselors, have specialized training and expertise in helping individuals overcome a wide range of challenges. They can provide insight into your child's behavior and help identify the underlying issues that may be contributing to their struggles.

Objective Perspective: Professionals can offer an objective perspective on your child's situation. As parents, we may have biases or emotional attachments that can make it difficult to see our child's situation clearly. A professional can offer an outside perspective and provide an unbiased assessment of your child's needs.

Evidence-Based Interventions: Professionals can provide evidence-based interventions that are tailored to your child's specific needs. These interventions have been shown to be effective in treating a wide range of challenges and can help your child make progress in their development.

Confidentiality: Professionals are bound by strict confidentiality guidelines. This means that your child's information and sessions are kept private and confidential, which can help your child feel safe and secure in sharing their thoughts and feelings.

Validation and Support: Seeking professional help can help validate your child's struggles and provide them with the support they need to overcome their challenges. This can help build their self-esteem and foster a sense of empowerment. When to Seek Professional Help It can be difficult to determine when to seek professional help for your child.

Here are some signs that your child may benefit from professional help:

Persistent or Intense Emotional Distress: If your child is experiencing persistent or intense emotional distress, such as anxiety, depression, or anger, it may be time to seek professional help.

Behavioral Issues: If your child is exhibiting behavioral issues, such as aggression, defiance, or withdrawal, it may be a sign that they need professional support.

Developmental Delays: If your child is experiencing developmental delays in areas such as language, social skills, or motor skills, seeking professional help can provide the support they need to catch up.

Trauma or Significant Life Changes: If your child has experienced trauma or significant life changes, such as divorce or the death of a loved one, seeking professional help can help them process their emotions and cope with the changes.

How to Seek Professional Help?

Talk to Your Child's Pediatrician: Your child's pediatrician can provide a referral to a mental health professional or counselor who specializes in working with children.

Check with Your Insurance Provider: Your insurance provider may cover mental health services for your child. Check with your provider to see what services are covered.

Research Local Resources: There may be local resources, such as community health clinics or non-profit organizations, that offer mental health services for children.

Ask for Recommendations: Ask friends, family members, or other parents for recommendations on mental health professionals who have experience working with children.

Contact Mental Health Professional Organizations: Professional organizations, such as the American Psychological Association, can provide information on mental health professionals in your area who specialize in working with children.

Seeking professional help for your child can be a difficult decision, but it can also be a crucial step in helping your child overcome challenges and thrive. Professionals offer specialized expertise, objective perspective, evidence-based interventions, confidentiality, validation, and support that can help your child make progress in their development.

It is important to pay attention to signs that your child may benefit from professional help, such as persistent emotional distress, behavioral issues, developmental delays, and trauma or significant life changes. If you do decide to seek professional help, there are a variety of resources available to help you find a qualified mental health professional or counselor who specializes in working with children.

By taking this step, you can provide your child with the support they need to reach their full potential and overcome their challenges.

Printed in Great Britain
by Amazon

25057145R00057